Bhakti Yoga Sutras

Teachings on Bhakti

Maha Visnu

Dedication

To Srila Prabhupada, whose vision of a house in which the whole world can peacefully live is based on the principles of Bhakti Yoga.

To my daughters Bhakti-Priya and Shanti-Priya, by whose memory I am reminded, every day, of the true meaning, challenges, and rewards of unconditional love.

For Mom, my spiritual North Star and who is the very embodiment of unconditional love, gratitude, and joy.

And

To Devi, with whom, walking hand in hand, I share this incredible journey of Bhakti Yoga.

Table of Contents

Introduction

1) Bhakti Yoga?
2) The Yoga Trinity: Karma, Jnana, and Bhakti
3) Anarthas & Arishad-vargas: Obstacles & Enemies
4) Wheel of Samsara
5) The Path of Dharma
6) Kirtan
7) Bhakti Yoga
8) The Five Bhakti Rasas
9) Guru and Satsang

Summary

Introduction

This writing on Bhakti Yoga is by no means exhaustive and it does not attempt to delve into the philosophical, practical, and spiritual depths of the ocean of Bhakti. Moreover, it does not attempt to act as an abridged substitute for, or compilation of, the voluminous writings on the subject of Bhakti Yoga. The purpose of this writing is to empower the aspiring yogi in their spiritual journey and development and to provide a launching point for further learning and practice in Bhakti Yoga. In a way the purpose of this book is not to answer questions about Bhakti Yoga but to give the reader the language, foundation, and frame of reference to know what questions to ask and how to query further into the nature and mysteries of Bhakti Yoga. If the reader comes away with far more questions than answers then this writing has been successful.

Copyright by Maha Visnu 2019

Bhakti Yoga Sutras

Chapter 1

Why Bhakti Yoga?

Why Bhakti Yoga?

1.1

Bhakti means unconditional, all-encompassing, eternal, and reality-based love.

Why Bhakti Yoga?

1.2

Yoga refers to unification or connection.

Why Bhakti Yoga?

1.3

Bhakti Yoga is to connect with and express our true spiritual nature through unconditional, eternal, and pure relationships of Suddha Bhakti (pure love).

Why Bhakti Yoga?

1.4

The goal of Bhakti Yoga is to fully develop this Suddha Bhakti (pure love) so that it is manifests in all three types of relationships: 1) Adhi-daiva, with the Divine, 2) Adhi-bhuta, with all creatures, and 3) Adhi-atma, with the self.

Why Bhakti Yoga?

1.5

When the jiva (individual spiritual being encased in a physical body) has developed Suddha Bhakti pure love manifests in all three types of relationships.

Why Bhakti Yoga?

1.6

The Sadhana (spiritual practices) of Bhakti Yoga leads to Suddha Bhakti (pure love); this enables the jiva (living entity) to achieve Moksha (complete freedom) and experience Prema-ananda (The joy of pure loving relationships).

Why Bhakti Yoga?

1.7

However, achieving Moksha (complete freedom) through the practice of Bhakti and experiencing Prema-ananda, cannot happen unless and until we are completely purified of the six Arishad-vargas.

Why Bhakti Yoga?

1.8

The six Arishad-vargas: Lust, Anger, Greed, Delusion, Arrogance, and Envy are obstacles that must be overcome to achieve Moksha (complete freedom). They are in fact the reason we do not spontaneously and naturally experience and manifest Suddha Bhakti (pure love) to begin with.

Why Bhakti Yoga?

1.9

Unfortunately, far too many are led to believe that one can attain and manifest Suddha Bhakti (pure love) without overcoming the influence of the Arishad-vargas.

Why Bhakti Yoga?

1.10

So long as we are compromised by the six Arishad-vargas we cannot achieve Moksha (complete freedom) and experience Suddha-bhakti (pure love).

Why Bhakti Yoga?

1.11

It is only with the achievement of Moksha (complete freedom) can one experience a full life of personal fulfillment, satisfaction, and joy.

Why Bhakti Yoga?

1.12

There are two types of Moksha: Jivan-mukti (freedom from the Arishad-vargas obtained while living in the material body), and Videha-mukti (freedom obtained after death of the material body).

Why Bhakti Yoga?

1.13

Jivan-mukti is Moksha that is achieved during our lifetime and results in our freedom from the Arishad-vargas.

Why Bhakti Yoga?

1.14

Videha-mukti is Moksha that is achieved after death and results in our freedom from Samsara (cycle of existence).

Why Bhakti Yoga?

1.15

When the jiva achieves Jivan-mukti (complete freedom from the Arishad-vargas) they gain the spiritual maturity and freedom to choose Bhakti. Because love can only exist where there is free will and independent choice freedom from the Arishad-vargas is an absolute prerequisite.

Why Bhakti Yoga?

1.16

It must be pointed out that even without achieving Jivan-mukti the jiva, by beginning Sadhana-bhakti (regular practices in Bhakti yoga), can attain to Jivan-mukti. Indeed, the practices of Sadhana-bhakti will ultimately lead to Moksha (complete freedom) and beyond to Prema-ananda (the joy of pure love).

Why Bhakti Yoga?

1.17

However, what is of absolute necessity in attaining and experiencing Prema-ananda (the joy of pure love) is freedom from the Arishad-vargas. The yogi who is compromised and bound by the Arishad-vargas will have neither the option nor the freedom to choose love.

Why Bhakti Yoga?

1.18

There is no more powerful and effective solution to challenges in the world such as poverty, suffering, and inequality than unconditional love.

Why Bhakti Yoga?

1.19

There is no greater antidote to sexism, racism, bigotry, violence, prejudice, and conflict than unconditional love.

Why Bhakti Yoga?

1.20

There is no greater power for personal, interpersonal, and social change, transformation, joy, and fulfillment than unconditional love.

Why Bhakti Yoga?

1.21

There is nothing, absolutely nothing, more difficult, arduous, grueling, punishing, excruciatingly painful, and rewarding than starting down the path of unconditional love.

Bhakti Yoga Sutras

Chapter 2

The Yoga Trinity
(Karma, Jnana, and Bhakti)

Karma, Jnana, and Bhakti

2.1

Our corporeal existence consists of three realities: physical, intellectual, and emotional. To attempt existence while negating and/or denying any one of these realities is to lead a handicapped existence.

Karma, Jnana, and Bhakti

2.2

These three realities of our existence, born of our Karma (actions and there resultant consequences) and Samskaras (impressions), exist seamlessly and simultaneously; thus giving rise to and manifesting our individual and unique character and experiences.

Karma, Jnana, and Bhakti

2.3

A healthy, wholesome human being simultaneously and seamlessly exists and develops his or her potential in all three realities of existence: physical, intellectual and emotional.

Karma, Jnana, and Bhakti

2.4

Atma-jnana (self-knowledge or self-realization) is having complete experiential spiritual knowledge, understanding, and mastery of these three realities of our existence.

Karma, Jnana, and Bhakti

2.5

The progress toward Atma-jnana (self-realization) is also threefold and achieved, in the yoga system, by the yogi's development in Karma, Jnana, and Bhakti.

Karma, Jnana, and Bhakti

2.6

Karma Yoga deals with the "whats" of our existence.
Jnana Yoga deals with the "hows" of our existence.
Bhakti Yoga deals with the "whys" of our existence.

Karma, Jnana, and Bhakti

2.7

While in truth all three yoga processes are interdependent and practiced simultaneously Bhakti Yoga, the "why" of our existence, is of paramount importance. This is because the human being is unique in that it is the only species that can ask and address the "why" questions of its existence.

Karma, Jnana, and Bhakti

2.8

The jiva (individual spirit being) should first deal with the "why" of their existence, the meaning and purpose. Thereafter the knowledge of "how" to live and align their existence and identity to their reality is addressed. Finally, the "what" essentially becomes self-evident; what lifestyle, choices, and actions are necessary to live to their full potential.

Karma, Jnana, and Bhakti

2.9

Many unfortunate aspiring spiritualists are guided to invert this progression and begin on the levels of "what" and "how" in their spiritual journey without addressing the "why". This results in a sporadic and haphazard spiritual journey where the aspiring yogi jumps from one process, religion, and philosophy to another without truly gaining traction in any.

__Karma, Jnana, and Bhakti__

2.10

We should first, and continually, address and engage the "why" of our existence, all else will follow.

Karma, Jnana, and Bhakti

2.11

The Atma-jnani (self-realized person) simultaneously and seamlessly lives, practices, and indeed has matured in all three yogas: Karma Yoga, Jnana Yoga, and Bhakti Yoga.

Karma, Jnana, and Bhakti

2.12

Unfortunately, many attempt to decouple these three primary Yogas from one another. This is as foolhardy and dangerous as attempting to decouple our physical, intellectual, and emotive realities.

Karma, Jnana, and Bhakti

2.13

Even though we begin our yoga journey by addressing and engaging the "why", all other yoga concepts and practices are seamlessly included.

Karma, Jnana, and Bhakti

2.14

The three yogas of Bhakti, Jnana, and Karma are the three spokes of the Yoga Chakra (Wheel of Yoga); with the jiva (living being) as the hub. All spokes are equally essential; the wheel is compromised without any one spoke.

Karma, Jnana, and Bhakti

2.15

However, while the yoga practices are engaged in simultaneously the spiritual maturation and realization of the yogi is like a ladder, it is sequential in nature.

Karma, Jnana, and Bhakti

2.16

This spiritual maturation and realization in Karma, Jnana, and Bhakti is tied to the yogi's spiritual growth from limited ego-centricity to all-encompassing, unconditional love.

Bhakti Yoga Sutras

Chapter 3

Anarthas and Arishad-vargas

Anarthas and Arishad-vargas

3.1

Anartha means that which is not wanted or required. In yoga an Anartha is an obstacle that prevents us from achieving our goal, Atma-jnana (self-realization).

Anarthas and Arishad-vargas

3.2

There are six major Anarthas (obstacles) from which all others grow.

Anarthas and Arishad-vargas

3.3

These six major Anarthas (obstacles) are called the Arishad-vargas (the six enemies).

Anarthas and Arishad-vargas

3.4

Kama (Lust) – In Vedic teachings Kama is far more broad and insidious than mere sexual desire. Kama influences us on 3 progressively more powerful levels: a) Thoughts – Initially we develop an erroneous belief that happiness exists in gratifying our corporeal impulses. b) Feeling – This initial belief becomes stronger and develops into an attachment. c) Willing – This attachment builds to an intensity that grows into a willing determination to act to achieve the objects of our desire. Moreover, this determination to act overrides our ability to discern, or even to care, whether or not there are unwanted consequences which we may accrue in the pursuit of satisfying our corporeal impulses. The senses can be temporarily sated but Kama, the energy itself, can never truly be satisfied and burns like fire.

Anarthas and Arishad-vargas

3.5

Krodha (Anger) – Krodha is born of Kama (Lust). Without Kama, anger cannot exist. Krodha arises for three reasons: a) when we are thwarted in fulfilling our desires, b) when fulfilling our desires comes with unexpected negative consequences, and 3) when we lose possession/control of our desired objects for sense gratification.

Anarthas and Arishad-vargas

3.6

Lobha (Greed) – In Kama (Lust) we are solely concerned with satisfying our corporeal impulses and when they are sated, even though temporarily, we cease endeavoring to gratify them. In Lobha (Greed) even when our impulses and desires are sated and we cannot possibly gratify them further our endeavor and drive to accumulate sense objects continues unabated. In Lobha we are no longer simply endeavoring to satiate our senses; we are endeavoring to gratify Lobha itself, an attitude of possessiveness far beyond the satiation of our senses.

Anarthas and Arishad-vargas

3.7

Moha (Delusion) – We are now saddled with an erroneous belief, an intense attachment, and a strenuous endeavor to accumulate for the sake of accumulation itself. Left unchecked a diseased mentality of entitlement is born where we begin to believe that achieving corporeal gratification and accumulating sense objects is our inalienable right. A deep ego-centricity becomes rooted in our being dictating that we have a near divine right to expect others to acquiesce and cater to our wants in all ways and in all circumstances. In this deluded state of ego-centricity we relate to people, objects, and circumstances only in terms of whether or not they cater to our corporeal impulses and desires.

Anarthas and Arishad-vargas

3.8

Mada (Arrogance) – Not far removed from Moha (Delusion) this quality moves us to ego-maniacal tendencies. Whereas in Moha (Delusion) we expected to always get our way, in Mada (Arrogance) we now demand it.

Anarthas and Arishad-vargas

3.9

Matsarya (Envy) – This is where aggression and violence is born. At this point we are well beyond merely attempting to satisfy our corporeal impulses and desires or amass vast amounts of sense objects. In fact it is no longer about satisfying our senses at all. At this stage we are unable to countenance another Jiva achieving personal satisfaction or fulfillment. Moreover, being compromised and overcome by Matsarya (Envy) we will, without hesitation, undermine or prevent another Jiva from achieving fulfillment. Before this stage we did not maliciously infringe upon the boundaries of others to achieve our sense gratification. Indeed, before this point we, in varying degrees, basically accepted and respected the boundaries and rights of others. However, in Matsarya this changes. Now compromised by Matsarya we actively, intentionally, and even aggressively, infringe upon the boundaries, rights, and lives of others without care or compunction.

Anarthas and Arishad-vargas

3.10

Bhakti (unconditional love) requires freedom. Without freedom love cannot exist. If the jiva is compromised by the Arishad-vargas it, needless to say, has no freedom.

Anarthas and Arishad-vargas

3.11

To master the Arishad-vargas is to obtain freedom. If we are enslaved to them we can in no way choose to create and maintain relationships of love.

Anarthas and Arishad-vargas

3.12

It is easy to see why these six Arishad-vargas are anathema to the development of Bhakti Yoga. Indeed, the Arishad-vargas are anathema to civilized life altogether regardless of one's spiritual inclinations.

Anarthas and Arishad-vargas

3.13

The Arishad-vargas take birth and reside in our Ahankara.

Bhakti Yoga Sutras

Chapter 4

Wheel of Samsara

Wheel of Samsara

4.1

Ahankara (false ego) is our identification with an incomplete understanding of reality. Reality has two dimensions: Apara-shakti (unconscious material energy), and Para-shakti (conscious spiritual energy).

Wheel of Samsara

4.2

Ahankara causes us is to identify with the Sarira (body), Indriya (senses), and Manas (mind); all of which are Apara-shakti (material energy and matter-based). This identification is devoid of any recognition or understanding of atma (the soul); that is Para Sakti (spiritual energy and spirit-based). This erroneous identification and understanding is Ahankara (false ego) and it handicaps our existence.

Wheel of Samsara

4.3

Due to Samsara (the infinite cycle of existence) the jiva has experienced numerous, even countless lives. Each of these lives has left layers upon layers of Samskaras (scars/impressions) upon the jiva; hence its Ahankara.

Wheel of Samsara

4.4

Each life leaves an untold number Samskaras (impressions) upon the Jiva.

Wheel of Samsara

4.5

Every newborn infant arrives in this world with an unspeakable amount of "baggage" from previous lives. This "baggage" consists of Samskaras, Vasanas, and Karma.

Wheel of Samsara

4.6

Samskaras (impressions) are created by our thoughts and experiences. Karma (consequence) is created by our physical actions. The act and experience of watering a plant produces both Karma (consequences) and Samskara (impressions) for the both the plant and us.

Wheel of Samsara

4.7

Not a moment goes by when we do not, in either thought, word, or deed, produce Samskaras and/or Karma.

Wheel of Samsara

4.8

Every thought produces a Samskara (impression) and we carelessly and haphazardly produce hundreds of thousands of Samskaras, whether slight or considerable, every single day.

Wheel of Samsara

4.9

These casually, impulsively, and whimsically created Samskaras in turn give rise to Vasanas (tendencies).

Wheel of Samsara

4.10

Past Vasanas (tendencies and proclivities) further impel us toward certain types of thoughts and acts thus giving rise to additional new Samskaras (impressions) and Karma (consequences). These new Samskaras and Karma in turn increase and intensify old Vasanas, as well as create new ones. This cycle is called Samsara (the cycle of existence). It is in this petri-dish of existence that the Arishad-vargas are born and thrive, and the jiva is drowning.

Wheel of Samsara

4.11

Ahankara feeds and thrives on these Samskaras (impressions) and Vasanas (tendencies) and uses them to create an incredibly powerful, though conditioned and entirely inaccurate, identity based on their aggregate.

Wheel of Samsara

4.12

Because this identity is created solely by an aggregation of accumulated Samskaras and Vasanas, that are based in Apara Prakriti (material energy), it is a limited and inaccurate identity because it does not include the jiva, that is Para Prakriti (spiritual energy).

Wheel of Samsara

4.13

Many spiritual processes are designed to arrest the production of new Samskaras as well as negate the effects of old ones. The idea is that being without Samskaras and Vasanas to which to cling and create an inaccurate identity, the Ahankara dissolves along with the conditioned individuality and attachments born of it.

Wheel of Samsara

4.14

Other spiritual processes are designed to engage us in acts and thoughts that produce pure and uplifting Samskaras. Such pure and uplifting Samskaras give rise to pure and uplifting Vasanas that in turn impel us toward more spiritually empowered acts and thoughts. What was previously Samsara (cycle of material existence) is now transformed into Yoga-rurukshu (an upward spiral of spiritual growth) toward Atma-jnana (self-realization).

Wheel of Samsara

4.15

The Ahankara, now with access only to spiritually pure and uplifting Samskaras and Vasanas, dissolves allowing our Svarupa (essential, individual, and spiritual identity) - which was previously buried under countless Samskaras accumulated over numerous lifetimes and suppressed by a fierce Ahankara - to reemerge and manifest itself in its full, unique, and radiant splendor.

Wheel of Samsara

4.16

Samskaras, and the way we generate them through thought and experience, have to be transformed. Ahankara (the false identity) which covers our Svarupa (full and complete spiritual identity) has to be dissolved.

Wheel of Samsara

4.17

Purifying Ahankara is no easy task. It is the single most difficult undertaking in our spiritual development. Indeed, this is the sole purpose of the yoga processes.

Wheel of Samsara

4.18

The purpose of yoga, all yoga, is to subdue and master the six Arishad-vargas.

Wheel of Samsara

4.19

By transforming our consciousness, and consequently, our Samskaras, Karma, and Vasanas, we can master the Arishad-vargas and dissolve Ahankara.

Wheel of Samsara

4.20

The battle begins with the Arishad-vargas.

Wheel of Samsara

4.21

The unfortunate irony, and our great misfortune, is that in the modern era we teach and practice "yoga" in a way that actually enhances and empowers the Arishad-vargas.

Wheel of Samsara

4.22

In dissolving the Ahankara, by mastering the Arishadvargas through the practice of yoga, we attain Atmajnana (self-realization).

Wheel of Samsara

4.23

Only on the level of Atma-jnana (self-realization), where our Ahankara is dissolved, can we experience Suddha Bhakti (pure love).

Wheel of Samsara

4.24

While some spiritual processes are intended to eliminate individual identity altogether, in short nullifying both their Svarupa (spiritual identity) and Ahankara (false identity), Bhakti Yoga does not seek this result.

Wheel of Samsara

4.25

Bhakti Yoga aims to create unconditional relationships of pure love based on total and accurate reality. Such loving relationships require a lover and beloved and can exist only where there is individuality, distinct personality, and complete freedom of choice.

Wheel of Samsara

4.26

By purifying our Ahankara and uncovering our Svarupa (true spiritual identity), we are able to live and experience, in this life, uplifting, fulfilling, unconditional, and fearless relationships of love.

Wheel of Samsara

4.27

We do not master the Arishad-vargas and regain our freedom by using our mental energy to directly engage and "conquer" them. We empower that on which we focus and engage. We subdue the Arishad-vargas and regain our freedom by focusing on and engaging their opposites.

Bhakti Yoga Sutras

Chapter 5

The Path of Dharma

The Path of Dharma

5.1

Dharma (principles of righteous living) comprises four basic principles. Cultivating lifestyles, habits, and ethos based these four principles leads to mastery of the Arishad-vargas, the subsequent purification of Ahankara, and the freedom, strength, and courage to choose unconditional love.

The Path of Dharma

5.2

The four principles of dharma are: Daya (compassion), Tapa (self-mastery), Saucam (purity), and Satyam (truthfulness).

The Path of Dharma

5.3

Daya (compassion) is practiced on both the Apara (material) and Para (spiritual) levels.

The Path of Dharma

5.4

Tapa (self-mastery) is to have mastery over the desires of the mind, urges of the body, and the impulses of speech. To gain mastery of the mind is to develop proficiency in Dhyana (meditation). To gain mastery of the urges of the body is to be regulated in habits of eating, sleeping, procreation, and work. To gain mastery of speech is to practice of Satyam (truthfulness).

The Path of Dharma

5.5

Saucam (purity) is to be clean both externally and internally. External cleanliness involves keeping our body, living spaces, property, and environment clean. Internal cleanliness involves keeping our mind clean of resentment, guilt, prejudice etc., and cultivating a mindset of generosity, patience, kindness, and gratitude. Moreover, Saucam encompasses a purity of motive. Knowing and purifying our motives are essential to living with integrity and realizing our highest potential. Pure motives are motives that are in harmony with the three categories of entities who inhabit universal reality: Adhi-daiva (the divine), Adhi-bhuta (nature and all creatures), and Adhi-atma (our own being).

The Path of Dharma

5.6

Satyam (truthfulness) is achieved when our communications are: Arjavam (factual), Priyam (pleasant), and Hitam (beneficial).

The Path of Dharma

5.7

Arjavam (factual) – Our communications are devoid of deceit and are based on complete facts as we know them. Priyam (pleasant) – Our communications are devoid of derogatory, inflammatory, demeaning or insulting remarks. Hitam (beneficial) – Our communications are based on the genuine best interest of all parties involved. These three facets taken together comprise Satyam (truthfulness).

The Path of Dharma

5.8

These four principles of Dharma are inherently part and parcel of the yoga system. Creating a life based on the four principles of Dharma is made possible through the practice of yoga.

The Path of Dharma

5.9

The most effective way to master the Arishad-vargas is to live and practice these four principles of Dharma.

The Path of Dharma

5.10

Where Dharma resides the Arishad-vargas cannot exist and our freedom is assured.

The Path of Dharma

5.11

Ahankara is only dissolved when the Arishad-vargas are mastered. Like a parasite the Arishad-vargas require the existence of the Ahankara for their sustenance. The principles of Dharma, as described above, master the Arishad-vargas and nullify the Ahankara.

The Path of Dharma

5.12

With the mastery of the Arishad-vargas, and the subsequent cleansing of the Ahankara, the manifestation of Bhakti in our existence begins to occur.

The Path of Dharma

5.13

To the extent we effectively align our habits, lifestyle, and character with the four principles of Dharma to that extent the Arishad-vargas are nullified and devoid of the power to control us.

The Path of Dharma

5.14

To live the four principles of Dharma - and overcome the incredible intransigence of the Ahankara, the massive weight of our Samskaras, the intense pull of our Vasanas, and the ceaseless onslaught of the Arishad-vargas - is extremely challenging. We cannot do it alone.

The Path of Dharma

5.15

The good news: we do not have to do it alone.

The Path of Dharma

5.16

To help us live according to Dharma; thus enabling us to develop in Bhakti Yoga and overcome Ahankara as well as the Arishad-vargas, is Krishna.

The Path of Dharma

5.17

As Partha-sarathi (a title given to Krishna and means "charioteer of Arjuna") not only instructed Arjuna in Dharma and the science of spirituality, He personally guided Arjuna's chariot through a host of enemies endeavoring to destroy him.

The Path of Dharma

5.18

The enemies the jiva (living being) is endeavoring to subdue are the Arishad-vargas and Partha-sarathi Krishna is the designated driver.

The Path of Dharma

5.19

Partha-sarathi Krishna guides and inspires the jiva to develop the strength and courage to choose a life of mastery over the Arishad-vargas consequently creating an uplifting existence of Suddha Bhakti (pure love).

The Path of Dharma

5.20

This partnership and bond between Partha-sarathi Krsna and the Jiva is enabled and sustained primarily through Kirtan (chanting).

Bhakti Yoga Sutras

Chapter 6

Kirtan

Kirtan

6.1

Harnessing and concentrating the incredible power of sound vibration and mantra, in order to transform and uplift our compromised consciousness, is the purpose of the Kirtan (chanting) principle.

Kirtan

6.2

Kirtan (chanting) is the recommended and most effective method in Kali Yuga (current age in Vedic cosmology) for spiritual development and reuniting with the Supreme in Bhakti Yoga. Kirtan can be practiced in two ways: Bhajan (singing meditation), and Japa (mantra meditation).

Kirtan

6.3

In Bhakti Yoga there are three prime Kirtan mantras that can be used in Bhajan (singing meditation) and Japa (mantra meditation): a) the Astakshara Mantra (eight syllable mantra), b) the Dvadasakshara Mantra (twelve syllable mantra), and c) the Sodasakshara Mantra (the sixteen syllable mantra).

Kirtan

6.4

The Astakshara Mantra is – Om Namo Narayanaya, "I offer respects to Narayana" (Krishna is also called Narayana).

Kirtan

6.5

The Dvadasakshara Mantra is – Om Namo Bhagavate Vasudevaya, "I offer respects to Lord Vasudeva" (Krishna is also called Vasudeva).

Kirtan

6.6

The Sodasakshara Mantra is – Hare Krishna Hare Krishna Krishna Krishna Hare Hare/Hare Rama Hare Rama Rama Rama Hare Hare, "Dear Radha Krishna, please give me loving service". The name "Hare" is in reference to Radha. The names "Rama" and "Krishna" are in reference to Krishna.

Kirtan

6.7

Radha is the Divine Feminine, Krishna is the Divine Masculine. Taken together they are the Divine Couple and epitomize and embody Suddha Bhakti (pure love).

Kirtan

6.8

The seven feminine qualities are listed as: Kirti (fame), Sri (fortune), Vak (fine speech), Smriti (memory), Medha (intelligence), and Dhriti (determination). Masculine qualities are equated to the four principles of Dharma: Saucam (purity), Satyam (truthfulness, Daya (compassion), and Tapa (self-mastery).

Kirtan

6.9

For the Jiva (living being) to realize its full potential the acknowledgement and development of both the feminine and masculine qualities, as defined above, are necessary.

Kirtan

6.10

Radha and Krishna are not only the divine embodiments of both the feminine and masculine qualities; taken together they are the very essence of Suddha-bhakti, pure unconditional love.

Kirtan

6.11

In Bhakti Yoga connecting with Radha Krishna is the most effective and efficient method of nullifying the Arishad-vargas, purifying our Ahankara, and enabling us to experience Prema-ananda (joy of pure love).

Kirtan

6.12

Of these three mantras it is only the Sodasakshara Mantra that includes the feminine divinity Radha and is therefore considered the most powerful of the three in Bhakti Yoga (and one of the reasons it is called the Maha "Great" Mantra).

Kirtan

6.13

The Sodasakshara Mantra, in combining both Sri Radha (the feminine divinity) and Sri Krishna (the masculine divinity), is considered the complete Bhakti mantra.

Kirtan

6.14

Japa (mantra meditation) can be done at any time, place and circumstance. Optimally, however, it should be done ten minutes each day, in the morning, and before the beginning of the day's activities.

Kirtan

6.15

Japa should be done in a quiet space while being comfortably seated. The mantra should be chanted out loud just above a whisper and Dhyana (our concentration) should be fixed on the sound of the mantra as we chant.

Kirtan

6.16

Improvement in Dhyana (concentration) is incredibly and exceedingly difficult as the struggling Ahankara refuses to die, refuses to let go of Samskaras, and continuously and valiantly strives to cling to its corporeal and false identity.

Kirtan

6.17

To improve one's Dhyana, continue to engage in Dhyana. Do not give up. Continue to focus on the sound of the mantra while chanting. With practice comes proficiency.

Bhakti Yoga Sutras

Chapter 7

Bhakti Yoga

Bhakti Yoga

7.1

The jiva, now engaging in the Sadhana (practices) of Bhakti Yoga, and unburdened by Ahankara, begins to manifest their Svarupa (natural spiritual identity). This Svarupa was there all along but suppressed by the Ahankara and subdued by the Arishad-vargas.

Bhakti Yoga

7.2

It is at the stage of realization of our Svarupa where we develop Suddha Bhakti (pure love). At this stage we now experience reality-based, pure relationships of love with Adhi-atma (ourselves), Adhi-bhuta (all creatures), and Adhi-daiva (the divine).

Bhakti Yoga

7.3

For the spiritualist who's Sankalpa (intention) is to merge into Brahman (the undifferentiated spiritual oneness devoid of relationships, individuality, and variety) the detailed Sadhana (practices) of Bhakti Yoga are not necessary. Adi Shankara Acarya's teachings on Advaita (non-duality) are excellent guides for spiritualists on that path.

Bhakti Yoga

7.4

Bhakti Yoga is Dvaita (dual) and requires two: Lover and Beloved. For spiritualists seeking to avoid relationships, individuality, and variety Bhakti is a poor choice.

Bhakti Yoga

7.5

Bhakti means unconditional love. In the Bhakti context love is synonymous with service. Therefore, service without love is slavery and love without service is not possible.

Bhakti Yoga

7.6

Love engenders service, and service is the tangible manifestation of love. Neither exists without the other.

Bhakti Yoga

7.7

When we love we naturally, spontaneously and joyfully desire to serve. The very service itself is its own reward and it gives us satisfaction, fulfillment, and meaning; this is Suddha Bhakti (pure love). Suddha Bhakti is love that is untouched by Ahankara and uncompromised by the Arishad-vargas.

Bhakti Yoga

7.8

The seed of Bhakti is in every jiva (living creature). The ability to experience and live an existence of unconditional love is part and parcel and, indeed, the very nature of the jiva.

Bhakti Yoga

7.9

This Bhakti-lata-bija (seed of the creeper of love), inherent in the very nature of all jivas, is obscured and covered by the Ahankara and nearly strangled by the Arishad-vargas.

Bhakti Yoga

7.10

The purpose of Kirtan is to purify this Ahankara, master the Arishad-vargas, and empower our innate ability to create, sustain, and experience pure unconditionally loving relationships in Bhakti.

Bhakti Yoga Sutras

Chapter 8

The Five Bhakti Rasas

The Five Bhakti Rasas

8.1

Bhakti (love) requires two, a lover and a beloved. Bhakti is interpersonal.

The Five Bhakti Rasas

8.2

Bhakti is universal, eternal, all-encompassing and limitless, and it is the inherent nature of the jiva. Our ability to manifest and share our reservoir of Bhakti is hampered only by our being overwhelmed and compromised, by the Arishad-vargas. Regain freedom from the Arishad-vargas and Bhakti rushes forth unabated.

The Five Bhakti Rasas

8.3

There are five basic Bhakti relationships: a) Santa (passive), b) Dasya (reverential), c) Sakhya (fraternal), d) Vatsalya (parental), and e) Madurya (romantic). These are the five Bhakti-rasas (loving "flavors" of relationships).

The Five Bhakti Rasas

8.4

Krishna is the only divinity, in Vedic theology, with whom we can share a unique, individual, and personal relationship in any one of the five Bhakti rasas.

Bhakti Yoga Sutras

Chapter 9

Guru and Satsang

Guru and Satsang

9.1

Sri Radha and Sri Krishna are the two, non-physically accessible, reservoirs of Bhakti from whom the jiva can receive the necessary nourishment, support, and empowerment in their spiritual life and journey. There are two, physically accessible, reservoirs as well.

Guru and Satsang

9.2

These two physically accessible reservoirs of Bhakti are Satsang (a spiritually supportive community of Bhakti Yogis) and Guru (a spiritually supportive mentor in Bhakti Yoga).

Guru and Satsang

9.3

Being supported by a Satsang (spiritual community) sharing the same Sankalpa (intention) provides powerful impetus and inspiration for continued growth and eventual success in Bhakti Yoga.

Guru and Satsang

9.4

The importance of keeping company with like-minded persons, in any area of life and particularly in the yoga processes, cannot be overemphasized. The very purpose of Bhakti Yoga is, indeed, the development of such loving relationships.

Guru and Satsang

9.5

As being part of a Satsang (spiritual community) cannot be overemphasized in its significance in our Bhakti Yoga development the same is true of having a Guru (spiritual mentor).

Guru and Satsang

9.6

There are two types of possible relationships one can have with a Guru. There is the Shiksa (student) relationship and the Diksha (disciple) relationship.

Guru and Satsang

9.7

In the Diksha (disciple) relationship the Diksha Guru not only teaches and guides the disciple but also vows and commits to accept responsibility for all past and future Karma accrued by the disciple. Furthermore, the Diksha Guru vows, no matter how many lifetimes it requires, to ensure all his/her disciples attain Suddha Bhakti.

Guru and Satsang

9.8

The Diksha Guru; being eternally responsible for the spiritual development of the Diksha disciple, as well as taking on their Karma, has undoubtedly mastered the Arishad-vargas and is firmly situated in Bhakti Yoga.

Guru and Satsang

9.9

In reciprocal manner the Diksha disciple promises, to the Diksha Guru, to adhere to the following six lifelong vows of ascetic and monastic living: 1) Celibacy, 2) abstinence from meat-eating, 3) abstinence from alcohol, 4) abstinence from gambling, 5) approximately two hours of meditation daily and, 6) lifelong submission to the guidance and instruction of the Diksha Guru.

Guru and Satsang

9.10

Breaking of the Diksha vows, by either the Diksha Guru or the Diksha disciple, carries grave spiritual and Karmic consequences for both. Because a powerful Sankalpa (intention) was broken, whether by the Diksha Guru or the Diksha disciple, the Arishad-vargas can be empowered and reinvigorated.

Guru and Satsang

9.11

Naturally the Diksha (disciple) relationship is suitable for very, very few and is best if taken, if at all, in the Vanaprastha Ashrama (retirement stage of life).

Guru and Satsang

9.12

In the Shiksa (which literally means "instruction") relationship the student commits to learn and engage in the Sadhana (practices) of Bhakti Yoga to the best of their ability. The Shiksha Guru in turn commits to teach, guide, and inspire the developing Bhakti Yogi to the best of their ability.

Guru and Satsang

9.13

The Shiksha (student) relationship does not demand adherence to the six ascetic and monastic vows of the Diksha (disciple) relationship.

Guru and Satsang

9.14

Whether one chooses the Shiksha relationship as a student or the Diksha relationship and becomes a disciple the importance of a Guru (spiritual mentor) is not insignificant. Indeed no worthwhile journey or goal in life can be undertaken or achieved without help, assistance and support from others. In Yoga the Guru (whether Shiksha or Diksha) is that help, assistance, and support.

Summary

To practice of Bhakti Yoga, purify the Ahankara and mastery the Arishad-vargas we can begin by following five Sadhana practices:

1) Refrain from meat-eating (promotes Daya)
2) Refrain from alcohol/recreational drug use (promotes Tapa)
3) Practice Japa 10 minutes daily with one of the three Bhakti mantras (promotes Saucam)
4) Find and join a Bhakti Yoga Satsang (promotes Satyam)
5) Receive support and encouragement from a Bhakti Yoga Guru.

The purpose of Bhakti Yoga is to uncover and develop our inherent Suddha Bhakti (pure love) within. This enables us to manifest it fully in relationships with ourselves (Adhi-atma), all others (Adhi-bhuta), and the Divine (Adhi-daiva) and thereby create an existence of spiritual and material balance, satisfaction and happiness and ultimately achieve Moksha.

Made in the USA
Columbia, SC
12 November 2020